PØPPEOPLE™

Lance Bass

by **Sarah Jane**

SCHOLASTIC INC.

New York   Toronto   London   Auckland   Sydney   Mexico City   New Delhi   Hong Kong

CONTENTS

iNTRODUCTiON

It feels like you've been waiting for this moment for practically forever, and it has finally arrived. The 'N Sync concert is right here, right now. So are you and your best friend . . . along with ten thousand of the luckiest people on the planet. Because unless you just got back from a really long trip to Bora Bora, you know that tickets for the 'N Sync concerts sold out faster than you could say Lance Bass (or JC Chasez, Justin Timberlake, Chris Kirkpatrick, or Joey Fatone).

The stadium is packed. The noise is deafening. Spotlights rove over the crowd as fans scream. The noise is earsplitting, and the concert hasn't even started!

The smiling faces of the five 'N Sync members

beam at the crowd from the banner that covers the stage. Then, suddenly, the banner drops away . . .

But wait! Where are the guys?

It takes a second to realize that they're *above* the stage, dangling from cables. Their bodies are limp, like marionette puppets. The song "I Got No Strings" from Disney's *Pinocchio* — a fairy tale about a puppet that comes to life — plays as the boys are slowly lowered toward the stage floor.

Halfway down they start moving in perfect rhythm (of course). They do look just like puppets! A few descending moments later they're all on solid ground and now grooving to the song "No Strings Attached" in amazing synchronicity.

It's all a little overwhelming — the music, the lights, the effects. There's no doubt about it: 'N Sync puts on a great show. Central to that super show is one particular 'N Syncer up on that stage. He's sweet, he's southern, and he has the greenest eyes you've ever seen . . .

He's the one and only mega-talented Lance Bass (pronounced like the fish, not the voice part).

Two songs into the concert, Lance steps up to the mike to greet the crowd. "Welcome to the No Strings Attached 'N Sync World Tour 2000," he says, his deep mellow voice carrying easily over the screaming crowd. "The next song we're going to sing for you best describes all of you fans out there tonight. We've been very blessed in our success these past few years, and we owe it all to you. So we dedicate this song . . . 'God Must Have Spent a Little More Time on You' . . . to all of you."

Wow. Not only did Lance introduce the concert, he introduced his — and possibly your — favorite 'N Sync song.

The guys step up to the mikes, your best friend waves her glow stick in the air . . . and the sweet harmonies begin. As the fivesome croons, you remember something Lance said about the song: "The words and melody are incredible. I get chills every time I hear it." When you close your eyes and listen to the music — especially the deep notes that Lance sings — you couldn't agree more.

Okay, so pretty much *everyone* knows that adorable Lance Bass — also known as Lansten or Scoop — is the blond-haired bass (a pretty cool coincidence) singer for 'N Sync, one of the hottest bands on today's pop scene. In fact, 'N Sync's album *No Strings Attached* — their second — holds the record as the fastest-selling album in *music history*, selling 2.4 million copies in its first week!

But back to Lance: Almost everyone knows

that he's in his early twenties and was born in a small town in Mississippi — and that he has gorgeous green eyes. But there's a lot more to Lance than those simple facts. This book covers *every little thing* about Lance, like *why* french toast is his favorite food and what his secret chat name is online. So if you want to know all of the teeny, tiny details about one very special 'N Syncer, you've come to the right place. This is the real Scoop, so read on!

Chapter 1

L'il Lance

James Lance Bass was born on May 4, 1979, in a small Mississippi town called Laurel. Located in the south-eastern part of the state, it has about 19,000 residents and is considered a quiet, community-oriented southern town.

Family Ties

Lance grew up with his mom, Diane, his dad, Jim, and his older sister, Stacy, who was three years old when Lance was born. Stacy declared early on that her baby brother was "a little doll." When she said that, she had no idea that twenty years later, millions of fans all over the world would agree!

The family was close. In addition to his parents and sister, Lance has always had a special bond with his grandmother. It was at her house that he acquired his taste for french toast — she made it for him whenever he slept over. FYI, Lance likes his toast the real French way: sprinkled with a little powdered sugar.

I'm Poo Fu

Lance says that as a kid he "was very hyper. I just loved to play and play." It's not too hard to imagine little Lance cruising streets with stately buildings and large trees. Lance was outgoing and funny, too. Everyone in his family thought he would grow up to be a comedian!

When he was little, Lance also spent a good deal of time with his uncle, who would one day give him his first job! The job was to dress up as a Dalmatian dog named Poo Fu, a character in a series of books called Poo Fu and the Gang. Lance would be Poo Fu at birthday parties and take pictures with kids to put in little storybooks. Poo Fu also played games and sang songs with the kids.

Lance loved — and still loves — animals. His family always had dogs, and when he was six Lance got his first pet pooch — a cocker spaniel named Goldie. And whenever he went to church camp, he rode a favorite horse called Old Toby. Lance was fond of Toby, which was lucky, because none of the other kids could control him!

When he was eleven, Lance moved to Clinton, Mississippi, which is farther north, a little bigger (population 25,000) than Laurel, and just outside the city of Jackson.

Making Music

And what about his introduction to music? There was some music in his house, of course. Lance was already plunking away on the family's piano by the age of four. Stacy and Lance also put on shows for their parents, complete with costumes!

Lance's real love of music, however, came from church, where his mom and sister sang. Lance says his sister "hated singing in public, but has a great voice." Diane Bass also sings, and Lance believes he gets his talent from her.

As for the introduction to singing in a group, Lance says it was his childhood friend Darren who first got him interested. The boys were in junior high when Lance joined the school chorus. At the time, Lance was already busy with sports like baseball, football, and basketball, and extracurricular activities such as Student Council, Fellowship of Christian Athletes, Youth in Government, Mayor's Youth Council, the Honor Society, and Students Against Drunk Driving. Plus he was Student Body Vice President. Whew!

Show Stopping

Still, Lance had time for more. He says Darren "was always singing. He wanted me to join a show choir, so I tried out and joined." Lance loved singing in his show choir, which was called the Mississippi Showstoppers Entertainment Troupe.

Before long he was also singing in a competitive choir called Attaché, which toured all over the United States. During Lance's stint with Attaché, the group performed tunes such as "Luck Be a Lady," "Ramblin', Gamblin' Man," and "Jump." Their competition show garnered them the local People's Choice Award and they were named Grand Champions of the Central Sound Classic in Indianapolis, Indiana.

While rehearsing, performing, and touring with Attaché, Lance also started working with a vocal coach — which proved to be fateful in the development of his career.

Reaching for the Stars

By the time Lance was fourteen, he knew he wanted to be a singer. But he wasn't sure he had enough talent to perform professionally. Besides, he still had a few other lofty goals in mind, like a career in space! Ever since he'd attended Space Camp at Camp Kennedy (near Kennedy Space Center in Florida) in seventh grade, Lance has been intrigued by space travel. He even took — and passed — the NASA entrance exam.

For a while Lance was torn between his two loves: singing and space. Which stars should he reach for? Fortunately for fans all over the world, the path became a little clearer before long. Lance was going to high school and working part-time in a day care center when he got an important phone call from his vocal coach. He was calling on behalf of fourteen-year-old Justin Timberlake. . . .

Chapter 2

Hook, Line, 'N Syncer

By the time Lance got the call from Justin, the rest of 'N Sync (Justin Timberlake, Joey Fatone, Chris Kirkpatrick, and JC Chasez) had already hooked up. Justin and JC had met on the *New Mickey Mouse Club,* and Chris and Joey were working together at Universal Studios. In a nutshell, it was Chris' idea to put a group together — one that would sing five-part harmonies. Chris called Justin, who called JC. Soon after that, Joey Fatone joined the group.

First Time Around

In the band's earliest days, there was another member who sang bass. His name was Jason. In those early days the guys were rehearsing hours and days and weeks on end without the guarantee of a record contract. It was a commitment that required a lot of time, a lot of devotion, and a lot of faith. Eventually Jason decided to go his own way.

For a while 'N Sync tried to get by with just the four core members. Joey tried to fill in the bass parts, but that didn't really work, since it's not his true voice part.

Hello, Lance?

Needless to say, the group knew they needed a solid bass singer — and they found the perfect one in Lance Bass. You might be wondering how the other guys found Lance in Mississippi while they were practicing in Florida. Well, Justin simply asked his vocal coach in his hometown of Memphis, Tennessee, if he knew anyone. Justin's coach recommended a kid he'd been working with, and they decided to give him a call.

The day Lance got the call to join the band he didn't believe the offer was for real. It was the day of his homecoming dance, and Lance was focused on that. It wasn't until the dance was over that Lance really started to think about the opportunity. He'd have to uproot and make the move to Orlando. Since he was only sixteen, and needed a legal guardian with him, his mom would have to give up her teaching job and move with him. And making it big seemed like a long shot.

Still, Lance decided to head down to Orlando. When he met the other guys in the group, they clicked. In fact, they clicked so much that Lance didn't even have to go through a formal audition. They sang a song together — something short and sweet — and that was that. Lance immediately knew he was in for the long haul.

How Do You Spell That?

There was one small catch though (besides leaving his home and friends at the age of sixteen). The name 'N Sync is more than just some cool name Justin's mom thought up to describe the guys' awesome singing and dancing synchronicity. It also happens to be an acronym.

Each letter in the name 'N Sync is the last letter of each member's first name, as in Justi*n*, Chri*s*, Joe*y*, and J*C*. Since the previous fifth member's name was Jaso*n*, the new member would ideally have a name that ended in "n." James Lance Bass didn't end in "n," but the nickname Lanste*n* did. So Lance's official band name, to his diehard 'N Sync fans, is and will always be Lansten.

At last the band had found a bass singer who jived with the guys and was ready to work hard despite some major hurdles.

In 1999, 'N Sync decided that their original record company, RCA, and the company that had arranged the deal with RCA, Trans Continental Records, were taking more from the band than they were giving to it. The boys wanted to move on to a label that would let them make more of their own choices. They chose Jive Records — the same label the Backstreet Boys and Britney Spears use.

But the transition wasn't easy. A huge lawsuit was brought against 'N Sync by Trans Con and RCA. The suit put 'N Sync's career and anxiously awaited second album on hold and even threatened to take away the band's name. Fans were up in arms.

In the end, the boys not only survived, they thrived. 'N Sync won preliminary hearings and the suit was settled out of court. During the turmoil, 'N Sync scrapped the album they'd been working on for RCA and did one on their own — their way — writing and producing much of it. The result is *No Strings Attached* — the best-selling album release EVER.

The five band members' chemistry and energy helped catapult 'N Sync to the top.

Going Solo

And now for a slightly touchy subject for Lansten fans: It's a hard, cold fact that Justin and JC get most of the 'N Sync solos. Joey gets his verses in here and there. And Chris not only sings the highest notes of all the singers — notes that are fairly easy to pick out — but also some lengthy solos. So when will fans get to hear Lance sing a solo verse of his own under the spotlight?

Well, to tell the truth, you probably won't. Unfortunately, songwriters just don't write solos for bass parts. In fact, bass singers are generally the unsung heroes of any group. While the higher parts have melodies that stand out, the bass part is often hidden underneath the other voices.

But take heart, because as any ensemble singer will tell you, it's the bass singer who keeps the group together and on key. The bass part is the part that the rest of the harmonies are built upon. Without the bass, a song lacks musical backbone. Without Lance and his fabulous low notes, 'N Sync would be sunk.

Chapter 3

in Tune With 'N Sync

You probably already know Lance's nicknames: Lansten, Mr. Cool, Stealth (he's been known to sneak up on a girl and sweep her off her feet — more on that in the next chapter), Poo Fu (from his first job), Shy Guy (only compared to the rest of the guys), and Scoop. But there's more info behind each name, and more to Lance than his names suggest.

The Scoop on Scoop

The nickname Scoop is one of the most popular, and was given to him by Joey's brother Steve, because Lance always knows what the scoop is.

In addition to being a low-note crooner, Lance has a talent for keeping tabs on everything that's going on in the schedule, from fan meet-and-greets to costume sessions to sound checks to concerts to interviews, which is obviously a lot! If any of the guys in the group has a question about what's going on when, Lance is the guy they seek out. He knows what's up and likes to keep things on schedule. "I don't like to waste time," he says. Who can blame him? With a schedule like 'N Sync's, Lance doesn't have very much time to waste!

Lance's organizational skills benefit everyone, but sometimes — like when the group is on tour — not even Lance can keep up. In fact, Lance thinks one of the hardest things about being on tour is "not having any time for yourself to get organized." And since Lance seems to be the one to organize the rest of the band, it's an extra-big job!

Shy Guy

Besides being the sensible member in the group, it's also been noted that Lance is more reserved than the other 'N Syncers. He's often described as the shy one and has been dubbed "Shy Guy." But as Lance puts it, "They're very crazy, so I wouldn't say I'm shy, but compared to the other guys, yes."

Still, Lance has had no trouble fitting in. His best friends "are the guys in the group," and he has bonded with "different bandmates at different times."

In the beginning, Chris and Lance roomed together and became fast friends. Joey and Lance could often be seen at clubs together, living up the nightlife. Lance and Justin also connect because they "have similar backgrounds and are almost the same age." And Lance says that "JC is fun to talk to about anything — he's very smart and intellectual."

'N Syncers on Lance

So, how do the other guys in the band feel about Lance? Chris notes that "he has a huge business mind," and Joey expands on that notion by saying that "he's really knowledgeable about business and marketing and is always on top of things."

This fact really came to light in 1999, when RCA was deciding which song on 'N Sync's self-titled album should be the second single. The executives at RCA were leaning strongly toward "For the Girl Who Has Everything." Lance, though, felt that "God Must Have Spent a Little More Time on You" would be a better choice. Lance convinced RCA to hold an on-line contest in which the fans could vote. Of course, Lance was dead on, and "God Must Have Spent a Little More Time on You" won as the obvious favorite — and became the album's second smash hit!

In addition to being a future music industry big-wig, Lance is known for being a great host. Justin says "he throws a great party," and Chris notes that "he took us all to his hometown and showed us Mississippi life at its finest." That's southern hospitality for you!

Lance definitely has a good relationship with each of the guys in the band. It's a good thing, too, because they're together all of the time, and could easily start to drive each other crazy. Amazingly, that doesn't seem to be an issue. As Lance describes it, "we're like brothers. Brothers always fight about nitpicky things, but you still love 'em." Even though he was the last one to join up with 'N Sync, Lance was clearly accepted from the start.

Getting in the Groove

According to Lance, the only real stumbling block for joining 'N Sync was that "I did not know how to dance. I was like, 'What? I can't do this. It's impossible.' I had to take it step by step."

Since moving in synchronicity is a huge part of the band's trademark, it was essential that Lance be able to get up to speed, and fast. So Lance worked one-on-one with a choreographer for hours every day. Another guy might not have been able to put in the time. Or have had the confidence to make it happen. But before long Lance was totally " 'N Sync" with the other guys.

These days, Lance is tearing up the stage with the other members of the band, bringing his own special moves to the show. One of the things fans love most about 'N Sync is that each of the guys has his own flair. As Lance puts it, "everyone has his own style." Chris is known for his crazy moves and flips. Joey has fabulous facial expressions. JC is always pumped up and jumping. Justin is smooth and funky — all flow. And Lance? His style is more like a professional Broadway dancer: hands out to the side or in front of him with his palms up or out. Pure class.

The Host with the Most

Lance has a reputation for being a great host, and he works hard to keep it up. When he makes it back to Mississippi, he says, "there are about two hundred people at my house — which I love, because I love all my friends." And sometimes, Lance throws a big southern barbecue, complete with hamburgers, hot dogs, and sausage. He reportedly makes a mean green bean casserole, and his all-time favorite dessert: Chocolate Dream.

Lance describes Chocolate Dream this way: "It's chocolate pudding and the bottom is a buttery pecan [as in his favorite ice-cream flavor] crust. There's a layer of Cool Whip, and grated Hershey's chocolate on top."

For fans who want to create their own Chocolate Dream, here's a recipe that comes pretty darn close to Lance's fave:

Chocolate Dream:
The crust ingredients:
1½ cups Pecan Sandies or similar cookies
6 tablespoons melted butter
Procedure:
1. Preheat the oven to 350 degrees.
2. Grind up the cookies in a food processor or with the back of a large metal spoon. Add the melted butter and stir.
3. Press the crust mixture into a greased or buttered pie pan.
4. Bake in the preheated oven for ten minutes or until golden brown.
5. Remove from oven and cool completely.
The filling ingredients:
1 package chocolate pudding mix (you ca_ use either instant or reg_ ular)
2–3 cups whipped top_ ping
1 chocolate bar
Procedure:
1. Prepare the puddin_ as directed on the pack_ age. Allow to cool if nec_ essary.
2. Pour the pudding int_ the baked pie shell an_ spread evenly.
3. Spoon whipped top_ ping onto the puddin_ and carefully sprea_ across the top.
4. Using a small han_ grater, grate the choco_ late bar onto the whippe_ topping.
5. Slice and enjoy!
Note: if you don't hav_ the time or energy t_ bake the pecan crus_ you can buy a ready_ made graham-cracke_ crust at almost any su_ permarket.

Chapter 4

Guess Who Hit the Small Screen?

He sings! He dances! He acts? If you missed the season finale of *7th Heaven* last spring, you definitely missed out, because Lance Bass guest-starred as Rick, Lucy's hot date!

7th Heaven is WB's wildly popular Monday night drama about the Camdens, a nine member family (seven kids, including twin babies) in which the dad is a reverend. It's an all-American slice of life featuring four teenagers.

In Lance's episode, Mary's parents won't allow her to go out on a date with Robbie, because they don't trust him. So Mary finagles the situation and gets her parents to agree to let her go on a double date, with her kid sister Lucy and Robbie's younger brother Rick (played by Lance).

At first, Rick and Lucy don't want to go. Rick already has a girlfriend, and Lucy isn't looking for romance. But when the two meet, sparks fly. They leave the movie theater early to find a better place to talk — and end up making out!

So how does Lance feel about being a guest star on the show? "I enjoyed it immensely!" he says. "I got on the set and everyone was so professional and so nice and really talented. I was very impressed."

When prodded, Lance also admits to being a little nervous at the time. "It's a lot harder than people think," he confessed, "with fifty people watching you and cameras everywhere. And I had to lose the southern accent. I had been in Mississippi for the last two weeks and it was really strong. I was supposed to be an Italian Californian!"

Lance, Camera, Action!

In spite of his jitters, Lance did a great job, and the *7th Heaven* director says Lance could have a future as an actor. Lance, for his part, has said many times that he loves acting — and that he thought he might become an actor before he got his big singing break. And it's pretty clear that this southern guy who grew up singing in church fit right in on the set of *7th Heaven*.

In fact, he fit in so well that the producers of the show have asked Lance to come back for at least two more episodes! In Lance's words, "I'll definitely be coming back next season. Rick will be coming back!"

Playing for a Million

In addition to playing Rick on *7th Heaven*, Lance had another television guest appearance last May, this one with Regis Philbin on ABC's popular game show *Who Wants to Be a Millionaire*. Lance was a contestant on the show along with such celebrities as Drew Carey, Dana Carvey, David Duchovny, Kathie Lee Gifford, Queen Latifah, and Rosie O'Donnell.

For a while it looked like Lance wasn't going to get past the fastest-finger round. Once he was under the spotlight, though, Lance did great. He answered 12 questions correctly (only three away from a million!) and won $125,000!

Of course, he didn't keep the money. Along with the other celebrities, his appearance on the show was to raise money for charity, and his winnings went to his favorite charity, Challenge for the Children.

Heading for the Silver Screen

Since Lance landed his role as a recurring character on *7th Heaven*, it's not all that surprising that he is looking into bigger acting challenges — like making a feature film! At the 2000 Cannes Film Festival, 'N Sync revealed that they have a movie in the works.

Titled *Why Can't I Be You*, the film is a high school story like *American Pie, Loser,* and *Boys and Girls.* The 'N Syncers will not be playing themselves, and the plot won't have anything to do with a band.

The boys are carefully considering who they will agree to make the film with. Tom Hanks's company, Playtone, is in the running, as is 'N Sync's own Phat Free Productions.

Now it's Your Turn

What would you like to see Lance in next?

Number your choices from 1-6, starting with what you'd like to see most.

_____ a stud on *All My Children*

_____ Conan O'Brien's sidekick

_____ a regular on *7th Heaven*

_____ Katie Couric's co-anchor

_____ an MTV veejay

_____ (your idea here)

What kind of movie would you like to see Lance and 'N Sync in?

_____ a drama like *Autumn in New York*

_____ a spoof comedy like *Scary Movie*

_____ an action thriller like *The Perfect Storm*

_____ a horror flick like *Scream*

Got No Strings

After 'N Sync disentangled themselves from their old record company, RCA, and their management company, Trans Continental Records, the boys branched out on their own as musicians and music producers. Their appropriately named album, *No Strings Attached,* is proof that they're better and stronger for it. Lance explains that *No Strings Attached* "feels like our real first album because we wrote and produced half of it. We are the executive producers of this one."

Taking charge has allowed 'N Sync to get to the next level. They have much more freedom with their new label, Jive Records. As Lance said, "We are in control of everything we do. Groups like us are usually all guided about and told what to do, and that is so not us. We are here to tell you we have no strings attached."

All the guys like having more control, but Lance, with his head for business, was especially ready to take the reigns. From the very beginning he has shown a special interest in all of the music business dealings and behind-the-scenes decisions that go into creating and maintaining a successful band. And it has paid off. Lance has already learned enough business savvy to be more active in the management of 'N Sync and to develop his own managing company.

Chapter 5

He's a Country Boy at Heart

So just what happens when you take a nice country boy and make him a megastar? Does he get starry-eyed and demanding? Does he forget the people he used to know? Well if the boy is Lance Bass, he remains true to himself, his family, and his roots and gives all he can to others.

Maybe it's because he grew up in a small town where "everyone knew everyone." Or because, as Lance points out, "my family keeps me down-to-earth. They would kill me if I got a big head." Or because his friends back home keep asking him, "Why do they act so crazy about you? It's just you!"

Or maybe he will always be a country boy at heart. It only makes sense. He grew up in the South — where country music has its roots, two-stepping is a popular dance, and horseback riding is common.

Heroes and Hopes

Whatever the reason, Lance's fame has not spoiled him, and his southern roots shine through in his heroes, hopes, dreams, and plans for the future.

Lance says his parents are his "biggest role models" and credits his success to them (along with the rest of his family, the other guys in the band, the crew, and his fans). And when Lance finally does get one of his rare days off, he usually wants to be "home with his family." Can you blame Lance's mom for being crazy about her kid? She's been heard saying, more than once, "He's the best son a mother could have!"

When it comes to music one of Lance's biggest role models is Garth Brooks. "Musically I respect Garth Brooks a lot, mostly [for] his [live concert] performances . . . He's the first where I went to a concert and said, 'That's what I want to do onstage.'" Lance also finds inspiration in Garth's unique personality, his positive attitude, and the way Garth enjoys his fans.

It should come as no surprise, then, that Lance has a particularly soft spot for country music. His first concert was Clint Black; he dreams of doing a duet with LeAnn Rimes; Lance even sings country songs in the shower. He has brought some of the other 'N Syncers around to appreciate the sound of country music, too.

'N love: James Lance Bass

'N tune: A rare shot of Lance at home, from 1996.

'N deep: Lance made a splash with
fans right away!

'Nch-by-inch

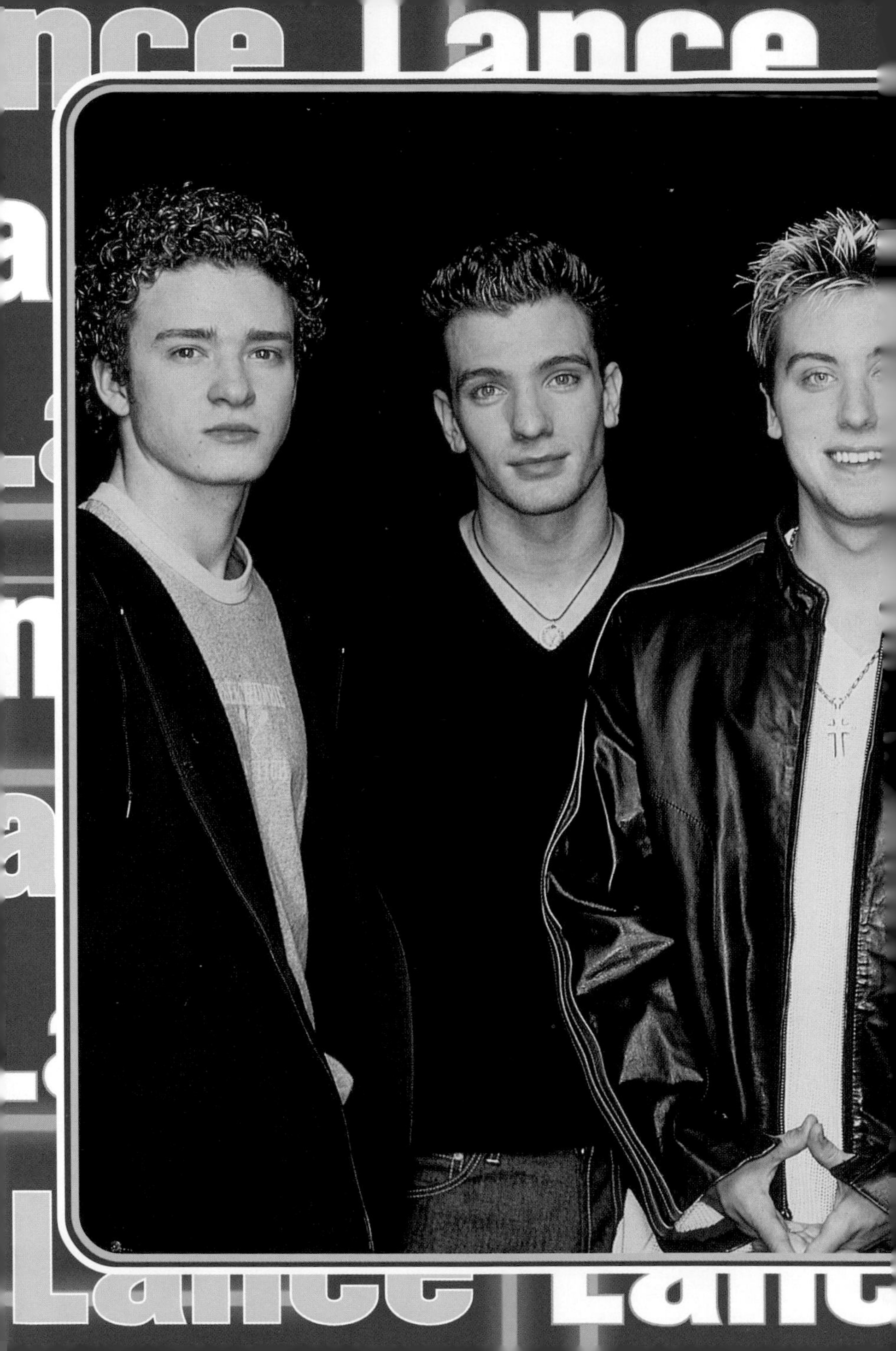
Lance
Lance

'N the middle: Lance was the last to join 'N Sync,
but first in the hearts of fans and his bandmates
(Justin, JC, Chris, and Joey).

'N concert: Lance has the deepest voice in the group, hence, he sings — you got it — "bass"!

'N pairs: Justin Timberlake is the natural fair-haired fella, Lance is the dye-guy.

'N store: The only strings on Lance can be found on his official marionette doll.

And it was Lance who brought Meredith Edwards, a country singer, on board as an opening act for part of 'N Sync's Summer 1999 tour.

. . . And Home Sweet Home

Before Lance made it big he wanted to live on a ranch in Mississippi with lots of land and horses. In 1999 he bought his dream house. Okay, so it doesn't have any horses. And while it was being renovated he told fans, "It looks condemned." But now that it's finished Lance loves it. "It's everything I wanted in a house," he said after actually living there for just one week.

The new place is filled with things to help him unwind and get away from it all when he's not traveling. He's got a virtual reality pinball machine and has even built a lake in the back so he can jet ski on his two SeaDoos!

Still, Lance never leaves the restrictions of fame behind completely. Before his house was finished he had to build gates to maintain security. He hadn't even set foot inside before people were flocking to see the spot where Lance was settling down. So much for privacy!

Lance recognizes that fame comes with a price, and he's more than happy to pay it. He's extremely grateful for all the fan support, and he participates in charity causes and events whenever he can find the time. He believes firmly in giving back, extending his hand, and using his fame to help others.

A Good Guy for a Good Cause

In spite of their busy schedules, Lance and 'N Sync have managed to do a lot of charity work over the past few years. Lance believes that charity work is important, and wants to help whoever he can (that's one of the reasons he started Free Lance Entertainment).

In 1999, 'N Sync founded Challenge for the Children (CFTC). CFTC's goals are to provide funding for schools that have suffered educational budget cutbacks for sports programs and music education. The foundation also tries to help with health care causes, such as adoption and foster care, teen pregnancy, alcohol and drug problems, and the fight against teen violence.

Last summer, Lance and the guys helped organize and played in the second annual Challenge for the Children Basketball Game in New York, which raised over half a million dollars for the foundation.

Though Lance isn't much of a basketball player — he was described as one of the worst players with the most heart — he loves the annual game because "it gets friends together to play basketball," and for a good cause!

In addition to the Challenge for the Children Foundation, 'N Sync has also made several commercials for the LIFEbeat organization, a national nonprofit AIDS/HIV awareness and resource group.

Lance and 'N Sync have also been spokesmen for the endangered white tiger by participating in the Stars in the Wild Project. The project produced toy white tigers to sell during the 1999 holiday season. A picture of 'N Sync was on each tiger's collar, and all of the proceeds from the toys went toward protecting the real white tigers.

Meet-and-Greet

With so little free time or privacy, you'd think 'N Sync would have given up doing meets-and-greets by now. Luckily for fans, they haven't. That's one of the special things about 'N Sync (and Lance, of course) — they are still grateful for all of the support the fans have given them over the years.

Lance has said it again and again: "We have the best fans ever. We can't stress that enough. They are the ones we do all this for, they are the reason we tour."

Whenever possible, Lance and 'N Sync have meet-and-greet sessions before concerts. They sign autographs and visit with as many fans as possible — answering questions, posing for photographs, etc. They also enjoy having fans backstage (and sometimes onstage!) to show them what goes on back there, which Lance describes as "All the chaos!"

Chapter 6

Lance Wants You!

It's no secret that Lance has a great head for business. As Chris puts it, one of Lance's best qualities is his "knowledge in business matters." With all of his talents, it makes perfect sense that Lance would want to pass on what he's learned in the music business to help up-and-coming artists. In a nutshell: That explains why he's started a management company called Free Lance Entertainment.

To use Lance's own words, "I feel so fortunate that I had the opportunity to do what I love. There are so many talented artists out there who never get the chance because they don't have anyone to help them. Free Lance will give that opportunity to a few phenomenal performers who otherwise might not have been heard."

Contrary to what you might think, Free Lance is

not Lance's first job helping talented musicians make it. Previously, Lance has also worked as a vocal coach and has always wanted to manage singers. "I've always wanted to be a manager, even before I wanted to sing," he says. "Managers *do* do good; they're not all just there for the money." Lance adds that his goal is to "see artists develop and rise to the top."

A Family Affair

As it turns out, Lance's new company is a family affair. Lance is the man in charge of Free Lance, and his mother, Diane, is vice president. Diane does a little bit of everything, from paying bills to consulting with Lance daily. Lance's sister, Stacy, is the artists' representative. That means she talks to the record companies on behalf of the talent. Lance's father, Jim, is in charge of the website and helps with contracts with the sponsors.

Calling All Talent

Lance already had two clients (Meredith Edwards and Jack DeFeo) when he held a contest to find new talent, too. Last summer, Free Lance held the "Outback Mountainboards Presents Free Lance Entertainment Search

2000." This search (dubbed Search 2000) was Lance's way of finding talent for his new record label. Entrants had to be at least 18 years old, and the finalists (and especially the winner) convinced Lance that they had what it takes to make it to the top of country and pop!

So what exactly were Lance and Free Lance looking for? "Well, the first quality is definitely the voice," he says. "It's going to be strict talent; I'm definitely going to know what I'm looking for when I see them on-stage."

To make it accessible to as many people as possible, talent searches were held in major cities all over the country, such as Dallas, Las Vegas, Atlanta, Orlando, Nashville, and New York. Lance attended as many of the searches as he could, but wasn't always able to be there due to his busy tour schedule. So Lance relied on Robin Wiley, 'N Sync's first vocal coach and writer and producer of many 'N Sync songs, as well as his mom to hear and consider a lot of the acts. Some of the other 'N Syncers also pitched in, including Joey, who helped out by listening to acts with Lance's mom in Joey's hometown of New York City.

Showcase Showdown

In August, MTV and Free Lance showcased the five finalists from its first talent search. The finalist performed on *Total Request Live* (TRL) all week, and on Friday MTV aired the "Free Lance Finals," in which each finalist sang part of a song for the MTV audience as well as three official judges.

The judges were Robin Wiley; the artist Pink (who opened for 'N Sync during its summer 2000 tour); and well-known R & B singer/songwriter Brian McKnight (who also writes songs for 'N Sync. Lance even admits he sings Brian's songs when he's in the shower).

The five finalists were all incredibly talented and had diverse backgrounds and musical styles.

The winner was a 21-year-old guy from Tulsa, Oklahoma, who taught himself to play the guitar in his late teens after being inspired by Dave Matthews. He performed an original folk-rock song called "The Look." His performance was phenomenal. As Brian McKnight put it, "This guy is a winner. If you don't take him, I'm taking him!"

The winner of the Outback Mountainboards Free Lance Entertainment Search 2000 won a record deal, and Lance says we should expect big things from him in the next few years.

Toro!

What's the craziest thing level-headed Lance has ever done? It has to be the time he volunteered to fight a bull in Mexico! It was his first trip to Cancún, and he went to watch a bullfight. The call went out for volunteers from the audience and Lance raised his hand!

The volunteers went into the ring, and after the first four guys got trampled it was Lance's turn to take charge of the bull.

"They put me out there with a little red cape and it came charging at me. Charged me like six times. It hurt a lot."

The bruises healed, but bullfighting is not something Lance will try again. Just ask his mom. "I think that after it was all over with, he realized that it might not have been a real good idea, but he wasn't thinking at the time. He survived — thank goodness."

Chapter 7

Lance on Romance

Imagine yourself on a date with Lance Bass. What could be better? He's cute, he's courteous, he's got that voice, and he's (in his own words) "a hopeless romantic."

Lance began practicing sweeping ladies off their feet at a very young age. He had his first girlfriend in kindergarten! And his first kiss ever took place with her in front of the whole school — at the South Jones High School homecoming dance where the two kindergartners were onstage to crown the homecoming king and queen. Lance explains, "I was the little crown bearer and she was the little flower girl. Since we were like boyfriend and girlfriend, they were like, 'Oh, they'd be perfect.' We had to take pictures and everything. Then I kissed her."

Lance started romancing early and still continues to do so these days, although he's not tied to a single girl. It's true that he has dated Danielle Fishel (she played Topanga in *Boy Meets World*) for about nine months. But since their breakup back in the summer of 1999, he's been footloose and fancy-free. In fact, he says he hasn't been on an official date since then.

Tough Break

For the record, though, Lance and Danielle are still friends, and their breakup was mutual. The two really cared for each other, but the long distance thing was tough — Danielle lives on the West Coast, and Lance was touring all over the world.

When they broke up, Lance says, "she understood, because she was in the business, too. But she was so busy and I was so busy that we hardly ever saw each other — like maybe twice a month. You just can't have a relationship like that."

No one knows better than Lance how tough his incredibly busy life makes it for him to have a real relationship. He says he misses dating, but that "it's not fair for the girl if you're always on the road. I can't stand dating someone and not being there for them. You can talk on the phone, but it's not the same."

Since Lance appeared on *7th Heaven*, rumors have flown about a romance between him and his on-screen flame Beverley Mitchell (that kiss *did* look awfully passionate!), but reportedly they're just friends. Whenever Lance is in Los Angeles, he and Beverley try to get together and hang out.

What a Guy Wants

In spite of his busy schedule, Lance says he sees himself settling down and getting married in the next several years. He wants a home and a family — he even imagines himself as a father of two kids. And the best part is that he isn't particularly looking to settle down with anyone in "the business."

So what is Lance looking for?

The first thing Lance looks for in a girl is "a great personality." His dream girl is someone he can talk to about anything — a best friend. In fact, Lance says he is usually friends with someone before they start dating. "I don't think I've ever dated someone who wasn't a friend first," he admits. "I always have to know them first, and then they become one of my best friends, and then we just start dating."

Lance is looking for someone to really share his life and his dreams. His perfect romantic partnership would be a lot like the song "Under My Tree," from 'N Sync's *Home for Christmas* album, which, as Lance says, "is about talking to your loved one. Talking about how you would make all your dreams come true just being with them."

Lance also wants to settle down with someone who is sweet and appreciates the simple things in life, like a home and a family.

So what does Lance's dream girl look like? Well, Lance tends to like blondes, but usually dates brunettes (and we're sure he wouldn't necessarily rule out a raven or redhead!). He doesn't have a set "type" in mind, but likes a girl who "cares about what she looks like but doesn't take it too far." He's not interested in "anyone who's too into themselves."

Dream Dates

Now that we've described the kind of girl Lance goes for, what about the kind of date Lance likes to go on?

Let's just say that Lance likes surprises. And adventures. Lance is into horseback riding, scuba diving, jet skiing, and bungee jumping. He also thinks that doing something with your date that she has never done before is a good idea. "You want to show them something different." And at the end of the date you can talk about it — it's a good icebreaking conversation."

Just like Rick on *7th Heaven*, Lance prefers a place where he and his date can talk instead of a night at the movies. "The movies is a terrible place," he says. "It's best to go somewhere that's not loud so you can get to know each other."

One of Lance's favorite places to go is the beach. After all, he *is* 'N Sync's official beach bum! So it makes sense that another great date for Lance would be a picnic on the beach to watch the sunset. But did you know that he'd be thrilled to cook all the food for the picnic? "I love cooking!" he says.

Chapter 8

Lance's Love-o-Scope

You know you like him. You've got the date all planned. But is your fave 'N Sync star in *your* stars? Before you head down to MTV studios to try and hook this Bass you'd better consult his astrological love profile — and yours.

Astrologically speaking, Lance is a Taurus born on May 4, 1979 — the sign of the bull. Taureans are hardworking, determined, and sometimes stubborn.

Although Taureans like material things, they're not fake or superficial. They are grounded and down-to-earth, and prize home and family along with life's luxuries.

According to *The Secret Language of Birthdays*, the exact date of Lance's birth, May 4th, is "the day of nurturing support. Those born on this day are destined to impart what they've learned through experience — they are dependable and there to help."

Consult the Stars

So, what about you? How would you fit in with this bull in sheep's clothing? Find your sign below and check out your astrological compatibility.

Aries: March 21th–April 19th

When a loving Taurus and passionate Aries meet, sparks fly. Lance is sure to like your adventurous nature. Skydiving, anyone? And if you tend to be too impulsive, a nice Bull boy like Lance could give you the loyalty, romance, and stability you need to balance your wilder side.

Taurus: April 20th–May 20th

Have you heard the joke about the ten-ton gorilla, the one that goes "Where does a ten-ton gorilla sit? Anywhere he wants to . . ."? Well, the same is true of two bullheaded Taureans. Hard work and commitment could take this relationship anywhere you wanted to go. But all that work doesn't mean it wouldn't be fun — you Taureans love to spoil each other as much as you love to be spoiled!

Gemini: May 21st–June 21st

You Gemini twins really are two people in one — and you might be too much for Lance to handle! One side of you would love Lance's down-to-earth nature and the nightly phone calls. But the other side would be ready to move on before you'd even settled down. If you can sit still long enough to take it slow and get to know the southern gentleman, the payoff would be a chance at long-term romance.

Cancer: June 22nd–July 22nd

Let's face it — Cancers can be crabby. But Lance's patience would help you smooth out any nasty disagreements. And if there's one thing that crabs and bulls always agree on, it's this: Nothing beats a quiet night in together.

Leo: July 23rd–August 22nd

Leos have a lot in common with Taureans, so if you landed Lance you wouldn't have any trouble understanding him. You basically want the same thing — to be completely adored! But watch your temper, Miss Lioness. Taurus isn't the only sign that can be bullheaded.

Virgo: August 23rd–September 22nd

Lucky Lance would do well to settle down with a Virgo. You devoted Virgos can appreciate his dedication, and he'd appreciate your quick mind and thoughtful treats — you love to pamper the people you care about. Plus you'd both prefer to take things slowly, which often results in a stronger relationship.

Libra: September 23rd–October 23rd

With the Libran's natural tendency to seek beauty and harmony in living, Lance could use a girl like you! Your attention to peace and balance would greatly benefit his hectic life. Plus, your elegance, charm, good taste, and kindness are all great assets for Lance's high-profile celebrity-studded world.

Scorpio: October 24th–November 21st

Scorpio, you are Lance's astrological opposite. Good thing opposites attract! Both of you are driven, which is fine as long as you're driving in the same direction. You might have to learn to compromise, but it would be well worth it. If you can decide on the destination, your differences will complement each other perfectly and bring you closer together!

Sagittarius: November 22nd–December 21st

Lance's 'N Sync lifestyle would suit you Sagittareans to a T. You love new places, new people, and new situations. And while you may not be looking for security, maybe Lance could teach you a few things about the beauty of stability and how to enjoy a (rare) calm moment.

Capricorn: December 22nd–January 19th

If Lance were to get together with a Capricorn, one thing is certain: They would not waste any time. You Caps are as efficient as Scoop himself, and your goals are set just as high. Success is practically guaranteed, but with intense focus like yours you definitely need luxury-loving Lance around to remind you to stop and smell the roses.

Aquarius: January 20th–February 18th

Aquarians are never boring. In fact your wild, spontaneous, out-of-this-world approach to life might just make down-to-earth and organized Lance throw his schedule out the window! While your different approaches could lead to conflict, the combination of creativity and dedication could also take both of you further than your wildest dreams.

Pisces: February 19th–March 20th

What a happy couple you and Lance could make, Pisces! Your caring natures complement each other perfectly. Talk about sweet harmony. And while Lance has what it takes to help you make your dreams come true, your gentle kindness and sympathetic ear are just what he craves after a hard rehearsal or a tough day.

Chapter 9

Lance at a Glance

Lance Basics:

Full name: James Lance Bass

Likes to be called: Lance

Nicknames: Lansten, Scoop, Pooper Scooper, Poo Fu, Shy Guy, Mr. Cool, Stealth

Birthdate: May 4th, 1979

Astrological sign: Taurus; the year of the sheep (Chinese astrology)

Birthplace: Laurel, Mississippi, USA

Parents: mom Diane and dad Jim

Siblings: sister Stacy and brother-in-law Ford.

Religion: Baptist

Ethnic background: English and Native American

Eyes: There's been some controversy about this — some say blue, some say hazel. True fans say, firmly and loudly: gorgeous green!

Hair: light brown with spiky bleached tips, and "so thick I can't style it!"
Height: 5′ 10″
Weight: 155 lbs.
Shoe size: 11
Pants size: 32, 32
Car: Black 1999 Toyota 4Runner

Faves:
Color: bright red and bright blue
Clothes: this changes with Lance's mood — he likes everything from his supercomfy pajamas to army gear to beachwear to sporty duds to full-on party style!
Food: Mexican and pepperoni pizza, along with french toast and Krispy Kreme donuts!
Soda: Dr Pepper
Ice cream: butter pecan
Jelly bean flavor: cotton candy
Getaway spot: the beach — with a picnic!
Superhero: Batman
Actors: Harrison Ford and Tom Hanks
Actresses: Lucie Arnaz and Jennifer Aniston
Modern-day author: Elie Wiesel
Classic author: William Shakespeare

Books: *The Outsiders; To Kill a Mockingbird*

School subjects: math and physics

Musicians: Garth Brooks (especially his performing style), Boys II Men

'N Sync songs: "God Must Have Spent a Little More Time on You," "This I Promise You," "Bye, Bye, Bye," and "Digital Get Down."

Video game: Bug

Cartoon character: Tasmanian Devil

Stuff to collect: Dr. Seuss artwork (his new house has a Dr. Seuss room!), old comic books, stamps, antique knives

Holiday: Christmas

Number: 4, 'cause "Tearin' Up My Heart" went to number 4 on the charts

Pickup line: "Do you believe in love at first sight or do I have to walk by you again?"

Part of being famous: the fans, and all the great people he's met

Least faves:

Lance is a pretty easygoing guy who looks for the good in all people and every situation. So the following list is pretty short. In a nutshell, Lance doesn't like:

1. people who prejudge you
2. people who don't listen
3. egotistical people
4. his Adam's apple — he thinks it's too big
5. mushrooms

Chapter 10

The Quotable Lance

Here are some fabulous, funny, and super-sweet quotes by or about Lance:

Lance on 'N Sync

"Everything we do is always together and that's what I think makes our group so unique."

"[Most of] the best days of my life have been in this group."

"We are happy beyond our wildest dreams, and even if everything was brought to a halt tomorrow we wouldn't be disappointed because we have so much already!"

[Our favorite pre-concert activity is] to hackey — it's been a ritual for us for I guess four years now."

"We're not a boy band. We're a dude band."

Lance on the tour:

"The bus is our home away from home."

"It was like *Real World*, except we all got along."

Lance on fans:

"We love our fans. I mean, the fans are what make us. We love spending time with them and meeting everybody. The fans are just incredible."

"Chat rooms are so cool, especially if you go into your own chat room and all the people are talking about you. . . ."

Lance up close and personal:

"I take a shower every morning and sometimes every night because I can't stand it when I'm dirty. I like to be clean. Mr. Clean."

"I can't bear looking in the mirror — I guess that's why my hair looks like this!"

"[In my suitcase] I carry my camera, because I take pictures of everything. And food, you have to have food. My watch that Joey gave me for my birthday . . . Playing cards . . . Taz . . . my Ricola because I have a cough all the time . . . and batteries."

Lance on fame:

"Sometimes I'll just be out onstage and say, 'When did this all happen?' It sprung up on us soooo quick."

"Everything is going great right now, so I must have done something right."

Lance on family:

"I always say to myself, is my mother going to approve?"

"My parents are my biggest influence. They tend to kind of rub off on you after living with them for nineteen years!"

Lance on life and dreams:

"I'm old-fashioned 'cause I'm from Mississippi."

"When I settle down, I'm definitely going to go somewhere in the country. Where there's a lot of land so I can have my own ranch."

"Have fun and live it up."

"Happiness is the freedom to do what you want, and to make music that gives happiness to others."

Lance on romance:

"I want . . . someone that can baby me. I think everyone wants that."

"I'm southern, so, you know, I'm a gentleman. I open doors, I pay for everything."

"I like really quiet dates. Just me and her, not around lots of people: going to the beach or staying in and renting videos."

Chapter 11

Did Ya Know?

Most fans know the basics: that Lance was born and grew up in Mississippi, that he sings bass, that his birthday is May 4th, and that his favorite foods are Mexican and french toast. But here are a few lesser-known facts and a few funny stories about Lance Bass:

- Lance was born at 1:20 p.m.
- He plays the keyboard, and started plunking the ivory keys at the age of four.
- Lance's first pet was a cocker spaniel named Goldie, who he got when he was in first grade.
- Lance has a tiny scar over his left eye that he got when he was little. He was playing American Gladiator with a friend who whacked him in the head with a broom. A trip to the emergency room and about seven stitches were the result.

- He had braces for three years.
- Lance was named "friendliest" in his high school class. He says, "I never wanted an enemy, so I tried to be friends with everybody. One night I'd go out with this clique, the next night I'd go out with another."
- He worked in a snow cone factory, and once tried to cover up a bug that flew into a cone he was making because so many customers were watching.
- He likes to wear white socks.
- He has a passion for Krispy Kreme donuts, and stocked his dressing room at Madison Square Garden in New York City with five dozen of the sugar-coated delectables. He plans to open a Krispy Kreme shop in Orlando with one of his bodyguards.
- Lance is a big fan of Katie Couric, the cheerful host on the *Today* show.
- Lance can't sleep if there's any light anywhere nearby . . . not even the little tiny light on his cell phone.
- More on the sleep thing: Lance likes to sleep on his side with one leg in and one leg out from under the covers.
- His secret on-line chat name is "impoofu."
- Lance believes that the secret to his success is dedication and trust in God.

- Two shampoos frequently used on Lance's locks are Selsun Blue and Pantene Pro V.
- Lance has a slight heart murmur.
- His average monthly phone bill is about four hundred dollars when he's on the road (it can get expensive when you call home every day).
- Lance loves cozy flannel sheets.
- Lance and a group of his friends created their own Blair Witch Project in the woods in Nashville.
- In the summer of 2000, Lance bought a pet ferret he named Dirk.
- Lance and the boys in the band wear in-ear monitors to block out the high-pitched and deafening screams of appreciative fans. Without the noise buffers, the guys' ears were being damaged by the incredible volume.

Chapter 12

Lance Timeline

May 1979:
James Lance Bass is born.

1991:
Lance joins the school chorus and shortly after that the Mississippi Showstoppers.

1992:
Lance snags a spot in the Mississippi competition chorus Attaché and tours the country.

1995:
Lance gets a telephone call on behalf of Justin Timberlake, asking if he's interested in auditioning for a band that's starting up in Orlando, Florida. Lance immedi-

ately hits it off with the guys in the band and joins 'N Sync as their bass singer.

1996:
Lance and the guys are signed to RCA/BMG Germany and take off for a tour of Europe.

1997:
'N Sync, the album, is released in Europe. The first single, "I Want You Back," goes gold within three months!

Lance and 'N Sync sing to sold-out crowds in the United Kingdom, Mexico, South Africa, Asia, and Germany.

1998:
Spring:
'N Sync returns to America and releases their self-titled album. "I Want You Back" is the first single.

Summer:
'N Sync's concert airs on the Disney Channel and propels Lance and the boys to overnight stardom. Their album goes platinum and hits the Billboard charts at number nine, steadily rising over the next few months.

Fall/Winter:

Lance and 'N Sync open for Janet Jackson's "The Velvet Rope" tour. Lance describes Janet as "one of the nicest persons in the world."

'N Sync appears on *The Tonight Show with Jay Leno,* and Lance offers to show Jay some dance moves.

'N Sync releases its holiday album, *Home for Christmas,* which contains Lance's favorite Christmas carol, "O Holy Night." *Home for Christmas* quickly joins their debut album on the Billboard top ten.

Lance and 'N Sync win Best Dance Clip and Best New Artist at the Billboard Awards.

Lance's (and lots of on-line fans') favorite 'N Sync song, "God Must Have Spent a Little More Time on You," is released as a single.

'N Sync kicks off their first headlining United States tour in Orlando, Florida, with Britney Spears as their opening act.

Lance and the guys ride on the M&M's Float during the Macy's Thanksgiving Day Parade, a big thrill for Lance because he had ritually watched the parade at his grandmother's house.

1999:
Winter:
Lance and the guys win Best New Artist at the American Music Awards. The award is one of Lance's most prized possessions.

'N Sync is a guest on *The Rosie O'Donnell Show*. Lance confesses, "It was a dream come true. She is like my favorite person in the world."

Spring:
It's back on the road — 'N Sync starts their new tour and plays almost every night in March, April, and May to sold-out crowds with opening acts that included Tatyana Ali, Sugar Hill Gang, Blaque, and B*Witched. Lance wore the bracelet given to him by Sugar Hill Gang for months after the tour.

'N Sync teams up with Phil Collins, who Lance says is "very great, and very down-to-earth," to do a track for Disney's *Tarzan*.

Lance and 'N Sync are immortalized on a foreign postage stamp!

Summer:
Lance buys a house in Mississippi and begins renovating it.

'N Sync hosts a charity basketball game in Atlanta, Georgia, to raise money for children's hospitals. Lance declares that "I will play basketball, but I am so bad they will make fun of me, but I like to try things."

Lance and 'N Sync make the decision to leave RCA Records and BMG in search of more creative control, striking a deal with the Zomba Records label called Jive. Shortly thereafter, Lou Pearlman and BMG sue 'N Sync for $150 million.

Fall/Winter:
The guys dude up and ride onto the stage at The Grand Ole Opry House to perform "God Must Have Spent" with Alabama, who recorded a cover version of the song (featuring the guys on backup vocals) in June on their *20th Century* album. Lance always *thought* that song could be a great country hit!

Lance and 'N Sync appear on MTV's *Total Request Live* with Gloria Estefan and shut down Times Square.

'N Sync is announced as guest vocalist on Rosie O'Donnell's *A Rosie Christmas* album. Lance, of course, is thrilled.

'N Sync performs "Bye, Bye, Bye" for the first time on television at the WB (the network that airs *7th Heaven*) Radio Music Awards.

For the September 1999 Video Music Awards, Lance and 'N Sync team up with Britney Spears. The guys sit at their desks like good students on her schoolroom set while she sings " . . . Baby One More Time," before launching into "Tearin' Up My Heart" — the single that is nominated for the Best Pop Video, Best Group Video, and Viewer's Choice awards.

'N Sync settles their suit with Lou Pearlman and RCA. Lance comments, "We're not puppets on a string, we control our own business, we've finally taken control of 'N Sync, and we're happy."

Lance and the rest of 'N Sync go to Hawaii — one of Lance's favorite places because it's loaded with beaches — to ring in the millennium (giving a sold-out concert, of course!).

2000:

Winter:

'N Sync hosts MTV's *Total Request Live*.

Lance guest-stars on *7th Heaven*.

'N Sync are presenters at the Forty-second Annual Grammy Awards Show and are twice nominated. "Music of My Heart" is up for Best Pop Collaboration and "God Must Have Spent" with Alabama is up for Best Country Collaboration with Vocals.

Lance and the boys return to *The Rosie O'Donnell Show* — Lance has a chance to catch up with his pal.

'N Sync is the musical guest on *Saturday Night Live*.

Spring:

'N Sync releases their long-awaited *No Strings Attached* album, which smashes sales records by selling over one million units in a single day. Lance tells reporters that his favorite songs on the album are "This I Promise You" and "Space Cowboy."

'N Sync teams up with Gloria Estefan at the 2000 Academy Awards to perform the Oscar-nominated "Music of My Heart."

Lance's uneaten piece of french toast (left over from a morning visit to New York City's Z100 radio station) is put up for auction on eBay — and sells for over a thousand dollars!

Lance and Joey head off to see the Bloodhound Gang show in Orlando, and Lance is mobbed by fans. (He later reported that at one point he was "scared for his life.")

On the set of 'N Sync's video shoot for "It's Gonna Be Me," Lance reports that he's still in shock over the success of *No Strings Attached*, describing it as "crazy."

Lance appears on ABC's *Who Wants to Be a Millionaire*, and raises $125,000 for the 'N Sync charity, the Challenge for the Children Foundation.

Lance spends Mother's Day in Nashville with his mom, where he announces the launch of Free Lance Entertainment as well as Free Lance's talent search, dubbed "Outback Mountainboards Presents Free Lance Entertainment Search 2000."

Tickets for 'N Sync's six-month, two-part *No Strings Attached* tour sell out in a single day.

Summer:
Free Lance's talent search auditions, set in major cities across the country, end.

Lance and 'N Sync are nominated for six MTV Video Music Awards for their hot video "Bye, Bye, Bye."

Lance willingly embarrasses himself in the Challenge for Charity second annual basketball game, this time at New York City's Madison Square Garden. (The tickets for this game sold out in fifteen minutes.) Lance and the rest of the players raise over half a million dollars.

Living Toyz announces that they will be producing a line of marionette puppets resembling the 'N Sync guys as they appeared in the video "Bye, Bye, Bye," and in the opening of the *No Strings Attached* tour.

MTV's *TRL* features spotlights on the five Free Lance finalists, and Lance himself cohosts the Free Lance Finals at the end of the week. The winner gets a record deal.

'N Sync and Britney Spears launch a CD and video campaign with McDonald's, Zomba Records, and Jive Records. Called *Your #1 Requests and More*, consumers are able to purchase an 'N Sync and Britney CD or video for $4.99 with the purchase of any regular menu item. The CDs and videos sold out in days!

Fall:

Lance and 'N Sync appear on MTV's Video Awards and give another fabulous performance.

Chapter 13
Discography

Lance and the guys have come a long way since they first got together in the fall of 1995. It's hard to believe that Lance was just sixteen when all of this started! He and the rest of the band have practically grown up before our eyes. As Lance points out, Justin "grew, like, two feet!"

What do the other 'N Syncers have to say about how Lance has grown and changed? Well, besides Joey harassing him about his old "bulb-head haircut" (don't worry — Lance got back at Joey by agreeing that Joey dresses even tackier than he used to!), the guys say that Lance has "learned a lot about music," and are impressed that he's managing other artists.

There's no doubt about it, 'N Sync has come a long way in five years, and has stayed together through great and difficult times. And with the release of *No*

Strings Attached last year, they showed just how far a boy band with a Mississippi bass can go!

Here are the details of the music they've produced to date:

NO STRINGS ATTACHED
Released March 21, 2000, worldwide.

1.) "Bye, Bye, Bye"
2.) "It's Gonna Be Me"
3.) "Space Cowboy"
4.) "Just Got Paid"
5.) "It Makes Me Ill"
6.) "This I Promise You"
7.) "No Strings Attached"
8.) "Digital Get Down"
9.) "Bringin' Da Noise"
10.) "That's When I'll Stop Loving You"
11.) "I'll Be Good for You"
12.) "I Thought She Knew"
13.) "I'll Never Stop" (European Bonus Track.)
14.) "If I'm Not the One" (European Bonus Track)

THE WINTER ALBUM
Released November 17, 1998, in Europe and South Asia.

1.) "U Drive Me Crazy"
2.) "God Must Have Spent a Little More Time on You"
3.) "Thinking of You (I Drive Myself Crazy)"
4.) "Everything I Own"
5.) "I Just Wanna Be with You"
6.) "Kiss Me at Midnight"
7.) "Merry Christmas, Happy Holidays"
8.) "All I Want Is You (This Christmas)"
9.) "Under My Tree"
10.) "Love's in Our Hearts on Christmas"
11.) "In Love on Christmas"
12.) "The First Noel"

HOME FOR CHRISTMAS

Released November 10, 1998, in North America.

1.) "Home for Christmas"
2.) "Under My Tree"
3.) "I Never Knew the Meaning of Christmas"
4.) "Merry Christmas, Happy Holidays"
5.) "The Christmas Song"
6.) "I Guess It's Christmas Time"
7.) "All I Want Is You This Christmas"
8.) "The First Noel"
9.) "In Love on Christmas"
10.) "It's Christmas"

11.) "O Holy Night"

12.) "Love's in Our Hearts on Christmas"

13.) "The Only Gift"

14.) "Kiss Me at Midnight"

'N SYNC
Released March 24, 1998, in North America.

1.) "Tearin' Up My Heart"

2.) "I Just Wanna Be with You"

3.) "Here We Go"

4.) "For the Girl Who Has Everything"

5.) "God Must Have Spent a Little More Time on You"

6.) "You Got It"

7.) "I Need Love"

8.) "I Want You Back"

9.) "Everything I Own"

10.) "I Drive Myself Crazy"

11.) "Crazy for You"

12.) "Sailing"

13.) "Giddy Up"

'N SYNC
Released May 26, 1997, in Europe.

1.) "Tearin' Up My Heart"

2.) "You Got It"

3.) "Sailing"

4.) "Crazy for You"

5.) "Riddle"

6.) "For the Girl Who Has Everything"

7.) "I Need Love"

8.) "Giddy Up"

9.) "Here We Go"

10.) "Best of My Life"

11.) "More Than a Feeling"

12.) "I Want You Back"

13.) "Together Again"

14.) "Forever Young"

'N SYNC

Released May 27, 1997, in Japan and Australia.

1.) "Tearin' Up My Heart"

2.) "I Just Wanna Be with You"

3.) "Here We Go"

4.) "For the Girl Who Has Everything"

5.) "God Must Have Spent a Little More Time on You"

6.) "You Got It"

7.) "I Need Love"

8.) "I Want You Back"

9.) "Everything I Own"

10.) "I Drive Myself Crazy"

11.) "Crazy for You"

12.) "Sailing"

13.) "Giddy Up"

14.) "More Than a Feeling"

15.) "Some Dreams"

16.) "Tearin' Up My Heart (Phat Dub)"

17.) "I Want You Back (Back Beat Edit)"

U.S. videos/ singles:

"This I Promise You," released fall 2000

"Bye, Bye, Bye," released summer 2000

"It's Gonna Be Me," released spring 2000

"God Must Have Spent a Little More Time on You," released winter 1998

"Merry Christmas, Happy Holidays," released winter 1998

"Tearin' Up My Heart," released summer 1998

"I Want You Back," released spring 1998

Chapter 14

Lance Online

We've given you lots of new information about Lance, but there's always the very latest news to read, the hottest pics to drool over, and the chance to get in touch for yourself. If you just can't get enough Lance, here are some things to check out:

On the web:
www.freelanceent.com
www.nsync.com
www.byebyebye.com
www.mtv.com

. . . or you can type Lance Bass into your search engine and see what comes up!

Where to send online fan mail:
impoofoo@yahoo.com

where to send snail mail:
'N Sync
Jive Records
137–139 West 25th Street
New York, NY 10011
or
'N Sync Fan Club
P.O. Box 5248
Bellingham, WA 98222